Longman Structural Read
Stage 4

GH00832076

Three mystery plays

Donn Byrne

EDUCATIONAL GUARDIANS

Tymawr, Llangorse
Brecon, Powys
LD3 7UE, U.K.
☎ 087484 383. Fax. 087484 363

Longman ⛵

LONGMAN GROUP UK LIMITED,
Longman House, Burnt Mill, Harlow,
Essex CM20 2JE, England
and Associated Companies throughout the world.

First published 1970
New edition 1981
Twelfth impression 1992

Printed in Malaysia by VVP

ISBN 0-582-52700-7

Contents

Bad luck!

Characters

Mrs Joan Ross
Mrs Dora James
Mrs Mary Green
Clara Clear, a fortune-teller

(In the sitting room of Mrs Ross's house. The three women have just finished their tea and are sitting talking.)

Mrs James: Oh, I almost forgot to ask you. Have you heard about Mrs Brown's daughter? She's going to get married!

Mrs Green: Who's she going to marry?

Mrs James: Oh, a young man from Australia.

Mrs Ross: Is her mother pleased about it?

Mrs James: She seemed pleased when I met her the other day.

Mrs Green: Where is her daughter going to live when she gets married? Is she going to Australia with her husband?

(At that moment the doorbell rings.)

Mrs Ross: Who can that be? *(She stands up.)* I'll just go and see.

(Mrs Ross goes to the front door. There is a woman outside. She is wearing a coat and she has a hat that hides part of her face.)

Clara: Good afternoon.

Mrs Ross: Good afternoon . . .

Clara: You seem surprised to see me. You *are* Mrs Briggs?

Mrs Ross: No. My name is Ross.

Clara: Does Mrs Briggs live here too?

Mrs Ross: No, I'm sorry. You've come to the wrong house.

Clara: I don't understand. This *is* the right address. *(She takes a piece of paper out of her handbag.)* Look, I wrote it down. Mrs Briggs, High Trees, Forest Road.

1

Mrs Ross (*looking at the piece of paper*): Yes, it's certainly the right address. But how did you get it?

Clara: Mrs Briggs phoned me. A friend gave her my name.

Mrs Ross: Why did she want to see you?

Clara: Oh, I'd better explain. I was going to tell her fortune.

Mrs Ross (*with some interest*): Oh, you tell fortunes...

Clara: Yes, Mrs Briggs invited me for the afternoon—but clearly I've wasted my time. (*Pause.*) Perhaps you'll let me tell your fortune...?

Mrs Ross: I...well, I have friends here.

Clara: That doesn't matter. I can tell everybody's fortune! And I'll make you a special offer. I'll charge the same price for all of you. Three pounds for fifteen minutes. That's all.

Mrs Ross: But my husband...he doesn't like this kind of thing. He'd be very angry if he found out.

Clara (*smiling*): He needn't find out. Don't tell him!

Mrs Ross: All right. I'll ask my friends. If they agree, you can tell our fortunes. Come inside, please.

(*Mrs Ross leads the way into the sitting room.*)

Mrs Ross: Oh, this is...

Clara: ...Clara Clear. I'm a fortune-teller.

Mrs Ross: Clara came here to see a Mrs Briggs. I've explained to her that Mrs Briggs doesn't live here, but she has offered to tell *our* fortunes...

Clara: Three for the price of one! My charge is three pounds for fifteen minutes. So if you agree...

Mrs Ross: What do you think?

Mrs Green: *I'm* ready. (*Turning to Mrs James*) What about you, Dora?

Mrs James: I don't believe in that kind of thing.

Mrs Green: I don't believe either. But it's fun. Come on!

Mrs James: No, I'll listen. I'd rather do that.

Mrs Ross: I hope Tom doesn't find out!

Mrs Green: Of course he won't find out.

Mrs Ross: Before we start, I'll go and get Clara a cup of tea.

Clara: Thank you. That's kind of you.

Mrs Ross: Please sit down.

(*Mrs Ross goes out of the room. Clara sits down.*)

Mrs Green: Why don't you take off your hat and coat?

Clara: I still feel cold.

Mrs Green: But at least take off your hat!

Clara: No, thank you. I always wear this hat when I tell fortunes. It seems to . . . help me.

Mrs James: But how can a hat help you?

Clara: I don't know. Perhaps it shuts off the outside world.

Mrs James: Hm!

(*Mrs Ross comes into the room. She is carrying a cup of tea.*)

Mrs Ross (*to Clara*): Here you are. A nice cup of tea!

Clara: Thank you. (*She takes the tea.*)

Mrs Ross: Don't you want to take off your hat and coat?

Mrs Green: I've already asked her. She says she still feels cold.

Mrs James: And the hat helps her to tell fortunes!

Mrs Ross (*sitting down*): Well, shall we begin?

Clara: Whose fortune shall I tell first? (*To Mrs Ross*) Shall I tell yours?

Mrs Ross (*to Mrs Green*): You have your turn first, Mary.

(*Clara takes Mrs Green's hand and looks at it with great care.*)

Clara: A very interesting hand! Now first I'll tell you something about the present. You have two children.

Mrs Green: Quite right.

Clara: And your husband . . . he works in a big office. In London. He's quite rich. I can see lots of money round him.

Mrs Green (*laughing*): Well, it's not *his* money. He works in a bank! But what about me? Tell me about my future.

Clara: Well, you're a very happy woman.

Mrs Green: Sometimes!

Clara: You like an exciting life. You like dancing . . .

Mrs Green: That's true. But what about the future?

Clara: Just a moment. It's not very clear.

Mrs Green: Oh!

Clara: But wait. I'll tell you all I can. You'll live for a long time. And you'll travel across the sea. Quite soon.

Mrs Green (*pleased*): She's quite right! I'm going to visit my daughter soon. She lives in America.

Mrs James: She's only guessing.

Clara: I'm not guessing. I *can* see into the future.

Mrs Green: Go on, Clara. Tell me more.

Clara: Well, your lucky number is five.

Mrs Green: I'll remember that. Is that all?

Clara: Yes. Don't forget your lucky number.

Mrs Green (*turning to Mrs Ross*): It's your turn now, Joan.

Clara (*to Mrs James*): I'd like to tell this lady's fortune. Then perhaps she'll believe in me.

Mrs Ross: Go on, Dora. Let her tell your fortune.

Mrs Green: She told *my* fortune quite well.

Mrs James: No. I refuse.

Clara: All right. (*She turns to Mrs Ross.*) I'll tell yours now.

(*Clara takes Mrs Ross's hand and looks at it for a long time. She does not speak.*)

Mrs Ross: What's the matter? Is it very bad?

Clara: No, I was just thinking. You haven't any children...

Mrs Ross: No, no children.

Clara: And your husband—he's quite rich.

Mrs Ross: You can see that from the house.

Clara: I'm not looking at the house. I'm looking at your hand.

Mrs James: What does Mrs Ross's husband do? Give us some *real* facts!

Clara: Let me see. I think he builds houses.

Mrs James (*pleased*): No, he doesn't! He sells houses.

Clara: It's almost the same. He makes his money from houses.

4

Mrs Ross: But what about my future? Am I going across the sea like Mrs Green?

Clara: No, you aren't.

Mrs Ross: Oh!

Clara: But I can see a house by the sea.

Mrs Ross: That's our new house. We've just bought it. Shall I live there for a long time?

Clara: No, I see you in another house. That one isn't by the sea.

Mrs Ross: Yes, my husband doesn't like the sea.

Clara: Your husband is a very strong man. He often gets angry.

Mrs Ross: He'll be angry if he finds out about this! What's my lucky number?

Clara: Three.

Mrs Ross: Oh, I thought it was ten.

Clara: No, that *isn't* your lucky number. Ten is unlucky for you.

Mrs James: It's the tenth of the month today!

Mrs Ross: Oh, is this an unlucky day for me?

Clara: Well, I can't tell you a lie. It isn't a lucky day for you.

Mrs Ross: Is my husband going to find out about your visit?

Clara: It's possible . . . (*She looks at the clock.*) Perhaps I ought to go. It's getting rather late, and I have a train to catch.

Mrs Ross: But you haven't drunk your tea. It's cold now. I'll get you another cup.

Clara (*standing up*): No, it really doesn't matter. I have to go now.

Mrs Ross: We must pay you. I'll go and get some money.

Clara: No, I can't take your money! I haven't told you very much about the future. It wasn't completely my fault. (*She looks at Mrs James.*)

Mrs Ross: But please take something!

Clara: No, I'd rather not. Perhaps I've brought you bad luck because I came here on an unlucky day. Who knows?

Mrs Ross: I hope you're wrong.

Clara (*walking towards the door*): Goodbye.

5

Mrs Green: Goodbye.

(*Mrs Ross goes out with Clara. She returns a few minutes later.*)

Mrs Ross: Well, what did you think of her?

Mrs James: It was a waste of time. She didn't tell you anything.

Mrs Green: Oh, I enjoyed it. And she was right about some things.

Mrs James: If I told your fortune, *I'd* be right about some things. But I can't see into the future. She was only guessing!

Mrs Ross: I hope she was wrong about today. I don't want my husband to know about this.

Mrs James (*standing up*): I must go. Thank you for tea, Joan.

Mrs Green (*standing up*): I must go too.

Mrs James: I'll take you in my car if you like.

Mrs Green: Thank you. (*To Mrs Ross*) I left my coat and bag in your bedroom, Joan.

Mrs James: And I left my coat too.

(*All three women go to the bedroom.*)

Mrs Green (*going towards the bed*): That's strange. My coat's here but my bag has gone.

Mrs Ross: Perhaps it's fallen on the floor.

Mrs Green (*looking on the floor*): No, it's not here.

Mrs James: And my coat's gone! It was on the bed too.

Mrs Ross: Someone's been in here. I . . . (*She goes to a small table near the bed.*) I left a ring here but that's gone too!

Mrs James: But how can anyone get in?

Mrs Ross: The back door was open. Someone came in that way.

Mrs Green: But when? I know that we were talking but we weren't making much noise. Why didn't we hear him?

Mrs James: Because you were busy with Clara. Now I understand!

Mrs Ross: I don't. Explain it to me.

Mrs James: Clara had a friend. While Clara was with us, he got into the house and stole our things. He knew he only had a few minutes, but that was enough.

Mrs Green: And so *Clara* didn't take our money. Her friend was taking it *for* her!

Mrs Ross: And she knew this wasn't my lucky day! What am I going to do? I'll have to tell my husband because I've lost the ring. Now he'll really be angry.

Mrs James (*rather pleased*): It was your own fault. You invited that woman into the house. She's stolen your bag and your ring. (*To Mrs Green*) How much money was there in your bag?

Mrs Green: About twenty pounds.

Mrs Ross: My ring was worth about fifty.

Mrs James: And what can you do about it? You didn't even see Clara's face! You haven't much to tell the police.

Mrs Ross: What about your coat? How much was that worth?

Mrs James (*smiling*): It was only an old one! I was going to throw it away. Oh! . . . (*She opens her bag and looks inside.*)

Mrs Green: What's the matter? Have you lost something?

Mrs James: The keys to my car. I left them in my coat pocket.

Mrs Ross: Then perhaps . . .

(*The three women rush out of the bedroom. They run to the sitting room and look out of the window.*)

Mrs James: It's gone! He's stolen my car!

Mrs Ross: Well, it wasn't *your* lucky day either!

The wrong man

Characters

George Shepherd, owner of the hotel
Mary Shepherd, his wife
Victor Penny
Joan Penny, his wife
Fred Grey, Joan's uncle
Inspector Bird
Radio announcer

Scene 1

(*A small hotel at the seaside. It is about a quarter to nine at night. It is raining hard outside. George Shepherd, the owner of the hotel, is in the sitting room with his wife.*)

George: Well, nobody'll come tonight. All our rooms will be empty again. How long is it since we had a guest?

Mary: Not very long. We had several guests . . . two weeks ago.

George: But the hotel hasn't been full once this summer.

Mary (*taking her husband's arm*): I know that business isn't very good, but don't worry.

George: It gets worse every week, my dear.

Mary: Perhaps we ought to sell the place.

George: But who'll buy a hotel that isn't making money? The hotel isn't in the right part of town—that's the trouble. It isn't near the sea and it isn't near the station.

Mary: And listen to the rain! Who'll come to the seaside if it continues to rain like this?

(*Just at that moment the doorbell rings. Mary opens the door and two people come in. The man is young and rather tall. He has dark hair and a fresh face. The woman is also young. She is very pretty.*)

Victor: Oh, good evening. We're looking for a room.

George: Well, I can certainly give you one.

8

Mary: Take off your wet coats. I'll take them into the kitchen and dry them for you.

Joan: Thanks.

(*Victor and Joan Penny take off their wet coats.*)

George: Any luggage?

Victor: Only this small bag. (*He holds up the bag.*) Our other luggage is still at the station.

Joan: We were looking for a quiet hotel. We were walking through the town when it began to rain. Then we saw your notice.

George: You've certainly come to the right place. It's very quiet here. How long are you going to stay?

Victor: I'm not sure. Several days at least. I have . . . some things I want to do here.

George: Can't I get your luggage from the station? It's no trouble, I've got a car.

Victor: No, it isn't necessary, thank you. I'll get it tomorrow. We're feeling rather tired and we want to go to bed.

Mary: Don't you want anything to eat or drink? Have a cup of tea!

Joan: No, thank you very much. We'd rather go to bed.

George: Then I'll show you to your room, Mr . . .

Victor: Jackson. Mr and Mrs Jackson. Do you want us to sign your book now?

George: No, you can do that in the morning.

Victor (*to Mary*): Goodnight. And thank you.

Joan: Goodnight.

Mary: Goodnight.

(*Victor and Joan follow George Shepherd out of the room. Mary turns on the radio. An announcer is just reading the news.*)

Announcer: That is the end of the news. Now here is a police message. The police are still trying to find Mr Victor Penny. Mr Penny left home two days ago. He is twenty-eight years old, tall, with dark hair. He is wearing a brown suit. His wife, Joan Penny, is also missing from home. The police believe that Mr Penny can help them in their investigations. If anyone has seen Mr Penny, please get in touch with the police. (*George Shepherd comes back.*) That is the end of the police message.

(*Some music begins to play.*)

George: What was the police message about?

Mary: The police are looking for a young man. They say he can help them in their investigations.

George: What's he done?

Mary: The announcer didn't say. He left home two days ago and nobody has seen him since then. His wife's missing too.

George: Is he a young man?

Mary: Yes. Why?

George: Perhaps it's the young man and his wife who are staying with us!

Mary: Don't say things like that, George!

George: Well, it's possible. They're young and they've come without any luggage. What's the name of the young man the police are looking for?

Mary: I can't remember ... something like ... Penny. What's the name of the man who's staying with us?

George: Jackson. But it may be a false name, of course. Did the police describe the young man?

Mary: Yes. He's twenty-eight years old, tall, with dark hair. Oh! Our young man was like that!

George: I told you! We get a guest but the police are already looking for him!

Mary: George, what colour was the young man's suit?

George: Let me think. (*Pause.*) It was brown. Why?

Mary: The young man the police are looking for is wearing a dark brown suit. It's the same man. What are we going to do?

George: Nothing! What *can* we do?

Mary: Oughtn't we to telephone the police?

George: Yes, we can do that. But we may be wrong. Then what will happen? If we've made a mistake, our guests will leave in the morning. Then our hotel will be empty again.

Mary: But I'm sure it's the same young man.

George: The world is full of young men who are tall with dark hair!

Mary: But he had the same colour suit, too!

George: *I* have a brown suit!

Mary: But perhaps the young man has done something terrible! Perhaps he's robbed a bank . . . or something worse!

George: Let's wait until the morning. It'll be in the newspaper and perhaps there'll be a photograph of the young man. Then we can be sure.

Mary: I'm going to take all our money to the bedroom tonight. And I'm going to lock the door of the bedroom!

George (*smiling*): Well, if he's robbed a bank, he won't want our money! He'll have enough already!

Scene 2

(*The next morning. George Shepherd is in the dining room. Mary Shepherd comes in.*)

Mary: Good morning, George.

George: Good morning, my dear. How did you sleep?

Mary: Not very well. I was thinking about that young man.

George: I didn't think about him at all. Ah, I haven't seen the newspaper this morning. Has it come?

Mary: I'll go and see.

(*Mary goes out of the room. She comes back with the newspaper and gives it to her husband. He opens it and begins to look through it.*)

George: Ah, here's something. The name of the man who is wanted is Penny.

Mary: That's right.

George: And here's a photograph of him. It isn't a very good one but he looks like the young man who's staying with us.

Mary: Yes, that's him! What's he done? Has he robbed a bank?

George: No, nothing like that. Some time ago they wanted to change the city centre of Linton. Some new plans were made and someone showed these plans to some businessmen. These men bought lots of shops and houses near the new centre and so they made a lot of money.

Mary: Was Victor Penny the person who showed them the plans?

George: They're not sure, of course. But he worked in the office where the plans were made. So the police think he can help them in their investigations.

Mary: What are we going to do?

George: Well, we ought to telephone the police.

(*At this moment Victor Penny and Joan come into the room.*)

Mary (*surprised*): Oh!

Victor: Good morning. You seem surprised. You hadn't forgotten about us, had you?

Joan: Perhaps we're too early for breakfast.

Mary: No, of course not.

Joan: We both slept really well and now we're ready for a good breakfast.

Mary: Good. I'll go and get it ready. It won't take long.

(*Mary goes out of the room.*)

George: Go and sit down at the table.

(*Victor sees the newspaper in George's hand.*)

Victor: Oh, can I have a look at that newspaper?

George (*giving Victor the newspaper*): Yes, here you are. There's something in it you ought to read ... Mr Penny! This report on page three.

(*Victor takes the newspaper. His face is very white. He looks at the report and the photograph.*)

Victor: There isn't much I can say. What are you going to do?

George: Well, you can have your breakfast. After that I'll have to telephone the police.

Joan: But Victor hasn't done anything wrong. He didn't show those plans to anyone. Please believe us.

George: Then why are you running away?

Victor: I'm not running away. I'm trying to find someone. I believe he's in this town.

George: Why don't you tell your story to the police?

Victor: They won't believe me. Everyone thinks I'm the man who sold the plans. I must find this person first—then I can go to the police.

George: Who is this man you're looking for?

Joan: My uncle. But we can't tell the police. They'll laugh at us. We must be sure first.

George: But how did your uncle see these plans? Does he work in the same office?

Victor: No, but—

George: I've heard enough. I can't believe a story like that.

(*At that moment Mary Shepherd comes in with two plates of food.*)

George (*to his wife*): This is the man the police are looking for, Mary. But he says he didn't do anything.

Mary: Well, have your breakfast. Then—

Joan (*to her husband*): You'd better tell them the complete story, Victor.

Victor: Are you ready to listen to me?

Mary (*in a kind voice*): Yes, of course we'll listen.

Victor (*sitting down*): It's like this. A few months ago my wife's uncle spent the weekend with us. We don't see him very often.

Joan: He's not a very honest man. He's often in trouble.

Victor: That weekend I took the plans home.

George: Wasn't that wrong?

Victor: Yes, but everyone does it. If we have a lot of work, we take it home and do it on Sunday. At that time the plans weren't quite complete. I worked on them on Saturday afternoon.

Joan: My uncle asked me: "What's Victor doing?" I told him: "He has to finish some important work." I said the wrong thing but I didn't think about it at the time.

Victor: Well, after I'd finished, I left the plans in the bedroom.

George: The plans were important. Why didn't you put them in a safe place.

Victor: The bedroom *seemed* safe.

Joan: And my uncle was with me or Victor. Except for about half an hour.

Mary: When was that?

Joan: On Sunday morning. I was in the kitchen.

Victor: And I decided to have a bath. Joan's uncle had finished reading the newspaper and was almost asleep. Well, I had my bath. When I came out, I went into the bedroom. I noticed my papers weren't in the right place. But Mary often moves my things, so I forgot about it.

George: But how could your uncle copy the plans?

Victor: In fact he didn't copy them . . .

Joan: My uncle's a photographer.

George: A photographer. So he went into your bedroom and took a photo of the plans. It's difficult to—

Victor: It's the only answer.

Joan: He had his camera with him. He takes it everywhere. It was in his bedroom. He had only to go and get it. How long would it take him? About five minutes.

Victor: When I went back to the sitting room, he was still in the same place. He seemed to be asleep.

Mary: But if this is true, why don't you go to the police?

Victor: But everyone thinks that *I* stole the plans. Will the police believe my story? Do *you* believe it?

Mary: Yes, I do! George, we must help them. Victor is right. If the police don't believe him, he'll go to prison.

Joan: Please help us. I don't want my husband to go to prison.

George: All right. I hope we're doing the right thing.

Victor: You are! You won't be sorry.

Mary: Finish your breakfast now. It's getting cold.

(*Joan Penny sits down at the table with her husband. They begin to eat. George and Mary Shepherd go into the kitchen.*)

Scene 3

(*The sitting room. Victor and Joan have finished breakfast. George and Mary Shepherd are sitting with them.*)

George: There are some more things I want to know. First of all, why do the police suspect you? Did they suspect you before you ran away?

Victor: Yes, they did. It's like this. All the other people in the office are older and more important than me. They did most of the work and then they gave the plans to me. After that I checked them. So I saw all the plans and papers. At one time they were in my charge. So of course they suspect me.

George: How did they find out that someone had made a copy of the plans?

Victor: I'm not sure. Perhaps they got the idea because people bought all the shops and houses near the new centre. I had heard about it but I didn't take much notice. Then the police began asking me questions. Clearly they suspected me.

Joan: Victor came home and told me. I immediately thought it was my uncle.

Victor: We also know he has a lot of money these days. He probably sold the photographs for several thousand pounds.

Joan: A friend of his told us. He also said my uncle was staying in this town. We have the name of the hotel.

Victor (*taking a piece of paper from his pocket*): The Sea View Hotel. Do you know it?

Mary: Certainly. It's one of the best hotels in town. But what do you plan to do?

Victor: We're going to set a trap for him.

George: What kind of trap?

Victor: I'll tell you. My plan is this . . .

(*There is the noise of a car outside the hotel. George goes to the window and looks out.*)

George: It's a police car! What can they want?

Mary (*to Victor and Joan*): They don't know you're here, do they?

Victor: Perhaps somebody saw us get off the train.

George: You'd better go and hide. Go to your bedroom and stay there. Don't come out until I call you. Don't worry. I won't tell them you're here.

(*Victor and Joan go out of the room. There is a ring at the door. Mary goes to open it and a policeman comes in.*)

Inspector: Good morning, Mr Shepherd. I'm Inspector Bird.

George: Good morning, Inspector. What can I do for you? I'm not in trouble, am I?

Inspector (*smiling*): Oh no, sir. We're visiting a lot of hotels this morning.

George: I see. Well, please come and sit down.

(*Inspector Bird sits down. George Shepherd sits in a chair near him.*)

Mary: Can I get you a cup of tea, Inspector? Or some coffee?

Inspector: No, thanks. I've just had a cup of coffee.

George: What's the trouble then, Inspector? Why are you going round all the hotels?

Inspector: You've probably read this morning's newspaper, sir.

George: Yes, I have. The news wasn't very exciting.

Inspector: Did you notice a report about a young man the police are looking for?

George: Was it about some plans?

Inspector: That's right. The plans for the new city centre of Linton. Someone sold a copy of these plans and the police are making investigations.

George: Well, what about it? Is that young man in our town?

Inspector: We believe he's here. A man says he saw him at the station.

George: Perhaps he has friends here.

Inspector: That's possible. But we think he went to a hotel.

George: Well, he's not here, Inspector. Our hotel is empty.

Inspector: I know you aren't hiding him, sir!

George: There was a photograph of him in the newspaper, but it wasn't very clear. Can you describe him to me?

Inspector: I can do better than that, sir. I have another photograph of him. (*He takes a photograph out of his pocket and gives it to George.*) Have a good look at that, sir.

George (*looking at the photograph*): I'll remember that face. He looks a nice young man. (*He gives the photograph back to the inspector.*) Do you think he's the man who sold the plans?

Inspector: Well, we're not sure yet, sir. But he ran away before the police finished their investigations. Perhaps he's going to try to leave the country.

George: Well, if he comes here, Inspector, we'll get in touch with you immediately.

Inspector: That's the idea, sir. (*He stands up.*) I'm sorry to give you this trouble.

George: That's all right, Inspector. It's your duty.

(*They walk to the door. George opens the door for the inspector.*)

Inspector: Many thanks, Mr Shepherd. Good morning.

George: Good morning.

(*The inspector goes out. After a short time they hear the car leaving.*)

George: Well, he's gone.

Mary: I'll go and call our young friends.

(*Mary goes out. She comes back with Victor and Joan. They all sit down.*)

Mary (*to her husband*): I told them not to worry, George. The police aren't looking for them here.

George: Now tell us about this plan of yours. How are you going to set a trap for . . .? You haven't told us your uncle's name.

Victor: It's Grey—Fred Grey. The plan's very simple. Joan is going to telephone her uncle. She's going to ask him to come here. When he comes, she's going to say: "Victor knows everything. He knows you photographed the plans and stole them. He doesn't want to go back to his job. He wants part of the money. Give us five thousand pounds and we'll leave the country. But if you don't give us any money, we'll go to the police."

Joan: Victor will be listening, of course.

Mary: But perhaps your uncle won't take any notice. What will you do if he refuses to help?

Joan: He *won't* refuse. He likes me. And when he sold those photographs, he didn't want to make trouble for Victor.

George: You'd better go and telephone. It's still quite early and your uncle will probably still be in the hotel.

Mary: The telephone's in the next room. I'll show you.

(*Joan and Mary go out.*)

George: But if your uncle doesn't come, what shall we do then?

Victor: Oh, he'll come. I feel sure of that. And he'll give Joan some money. But that's not enough. He must talk too.

George: We'll leave Joan and her uncle in this room. Then you and I can go into the kitchen and listen. It will be better if I listen too. The police will believe me.

Victor: You're right.

(*Joan and Mary come back into the room. They both look pleased.*)

Victor: Well, what happened?

Joan: He's agreed to come. He'll be here about eleven. I told him to ask for Jackson.

George: Good. The first part of the plan is complete. I hope the second part doesn't fail.

Mary: Don't worry about that. We'll win!

Scene 4

(*It is just before eleven o'clock. All four are in the sitting room.*)

George: Does everyone understand the plan?

Mary: Yes, I'll open the door and let him in. Then I'll call Joan.

Victor: Right. Mr Shepherd and I will be in the kitchen.

Joan: Then I'll come down and talk to my uncle.

George: Good.

(*The doorbell rings. Joan runs out of the room. George and Victor go into the kitchen. They do not close the door completely. Mary goes and opens the door.*)

Mary (*seeing Fred Grey*): Oh, good morning. What can I do for you?

Grey: I've come to see a young lady. Her name is Jackson. I'm her uncle.

Mary: Mrs Jackson? Yes, she's in her room. Please step inside and I'll call her.

(Fred Grey comes into the sitting room. He is about forty-five years old and is very well dressed.)

Mary: Excuse me, then. I'll go and call Mrs Jackson.

(Mary goes out of the room. After a short time Joan enters.)

Joan: Uncle! I'm glad you've come. *(She goes and kisses Fred Grey.)* Let's sit down over there.

(Joan and her uncle cross the room and sit down.)

Grey: What's the trouble then, Joan?

Joan: Haven't you heard? Victor's in trouble. The police are looking for him and he has had to hide.

Grey: But how can I help you? Victor oughtn't to run away like that. What's he done?

Joan: He hasn't done anything. People believe that he sold a copy of some plans—but it wasn't him.

Grey: All right. Perhaps it wasn't Victor. But how can I help?

Joan: We need money.

Grey: Yes, I can lend you a little money.

Joan: We need a lot of money, Uncle.

Grey: I'm not a rich man. You know that, my dear.

Joan: I met a friend of yours the other day. He said you have a lot of money at the moment.

Grey: I—

Joan: And you're staying at the best hotel in town.

Grey: It's true. I won a little money. And of course I never save. How much do you need?

Joan: Five thousand pounds.

Grey: Five thousand. But I haven't got five thousand pounds.

Joan: Oh yes you have, Uncle. You've got much more than that. How much did they pay you for the photographs?

Grey: What photographs?

Joan: The photographs you took of the plans.

Grey: Joan, my dear, do you believe this?

Joan: Yes, Uncle. Because it's true. You took photographs of the plans and you sold them.

Grey (*rather angry*): But it isn't possible. I never saw the plans. I don't work in Victor's office.

Joan: You came to stay with us one weekend. Victor brought the plans home that weekend because he had work to do. You went into our bedroom and you took photographs of them.

Grey: I...

Joan (*smiling*): It's all right, Uncle. Victor doesn't want to go to the police. He wants to leave the country. But for that he needs money.

Grey: Five thousand pounds.

Joan: It's not very much. How much did they pay you? Ten thousand pounds?

Grey: No, not as much as that.

Joan (*angry*): So it was you! You took the photographs and my husband got into trouble.

Grey: Please listen, Joan!

(*At that moment Victor comes into the room. Grey does not speak. He looks first at Joan and then at Victor.*)

Victor: Yes, it's me! I heard everything.

Grey: It was a trap! (*To Joan.*) You made me talk. I came here to help you and you did this to me.

Joan: You did worse things to my husband. He's had to run away from the police.

Grey: I didn't want to make trouble for him. I just wanted to make some money. Listen! I'll give you half the money.

Victor: I don't want it! I want to go back to my job. You must go to the police and tell them everything.

Grey: I won't. You can't make me talk. And perhaps they won't even believe your story. Come on, take half the money!

Victor: It's all right. They'll believe my story. You can come out now, Mr Shepherd.

(*George comes out of the kitchen.*)

George: Yes, I heard every word. And I'm ready to tell the police everything. It's no use, Grey. You're caught! You made trouble for these young people and now you must pay for it.

(*Grey suddenly runs towards the door but Victor jumps on top of him. Together they fall to the ground.*)

Joan: Quick, Mr Shepherd! You'd better telephone the police.

(*George goes into the next room. His voice is heard.*)

George: Give me the police, please. Yes, it's very important. Hello? Inspector Bird? Yes, it's me—George Shepherd. Can you come round to my hotel as quickly as possible? I've got somebody here you'd like to meet.

The case of the five-pound notes

Characters

Superintendent Keyes   **Mrs Cross**
Inspector Bright   **Woods**
Inspector Price   **Thomas Lamb**
Sergeant Driver   **A waitress**
Felstead   **A village policeman**
Lessing

Act One
Scene 1

The office of Superintendent Keyes in Scotland Yard. There is a map of London on the wall. Superintendent Keyes is sitting behind his desk. He is about fifty years old, with grey hair and a serious face. Inspector Bright is with him in the office. He is rather younger than the superintendent.

Keyes: I agree, Bright. We must act quickly before the same thing happens again. I'm putting you in charge of the case.

Bright: I shall need help, sir.

Keyes: Well, you have Sergeant Driver. Do you want anyone else?

Bright: Yes. Price, sir. He's the right man for this case.

Keyes: All right. He's rather young, but I agree he's a good man. I'd better speak to him.

(Keyes picks up the telephone.)

Hello? Is that you, Price? This is Keyes speaking. Can you come along to my office? Yes, immediately.

(Keyes puts down the telephone.)

Keyes: Does Price know anything about this case?

Bright: Yes. But he doesn't know all the facts, sir.

Keyes: Hm. Well, we'd better go over the case together.

Bright (*standing up*): I'll fetch Sergeant Driver, then, sir.

Keyes: Yes, we shall need him here too.

(*Bright goes out of the office. Keyes looks through some papers on his desk. He looks very worried. After a short time there is a knock at the door and Inspector Price comes in. He is young and very tall.*)

Price: Good morning, sir.

Keyes (*looking up*): Ah, good morning, Price. Take a seat. Bright has just gone to fetch Sergeant Driver.

Price: What's it about, sir? This stolen money?

Keyes: Yes. And we're rather worried about it. It isn't easy to get rid of stolen money but *somebody* has found a way.

Price: He got rid of more than three thousand pounds, didn't he?

Keyes: Yes, and all in one day. And there's still more money.

Price: How much, sir?

Keyes: About nine thousand pounds. So we must act quickly to find the person who is getting rid of the money.

Price: Have we got any clues, sir?

Keyes: Yes, we have a few clues, of course. We know the men who stole the money. We caught them and they went to prison for it. But that was fifteen years ago.

Price: But those men are all free now, aren't they, sir?

Keyes: Yes. And we can find those men without much difficulty. But this may be the work of someone who didn't take part in the crime. You'll understand that when Bright tells you about the case.

(*At that moment Inspector Bright returns with Sergeant Driver. Both men sit down.*)

Keyes: Good. Now we're all here. First of all, Bright, go over the story of the robbery. It happened before Price joined the police and he may not know all the facts.

(*Superintendent Keyes takes out his pipe and lights it.*)

Scene 2

(Inspector Price and Sergeant Driver are watching Inspector Bright.)

Bright: Well, the crime took place in 1970. The bank that was robbed was in the city. Forty thousand pounds was stolen and the money was all in five-pound notes. Four men took part in the robbery. Two of the men went into the bank and stole the money. It was ten o'clock in the morning and the bank was almost empty. They had planned the robbery well.

Price: But how was it possible to walk out of the bank with forty thousand pounds—even at ten o'clock in the morning?

Bright *(smiling)*: I'll explain in a moment. The two men who went into the bank were Lessing and George Felstead. The third man was Felstead's younger brother, Jack. He waited in a car, near the bank, and when his brother and Lessing rushed out with the money, he drove up. They jumped into the car and drove away.

Keyes *(taking his pipe out of his mouth)*: You were the man who arrested Jack Felstead, weren't you, Sergeant Driver?

Driver: Yes, sir. We caught him the following day.

Price: What about the fourth man? What did he do?

Bright: That was Cross. He was the man who planned the crime. He worked in the bank and he knew all about this money. Large amounts of money like that were only there on certain days. Cross was able to tell the others. But he also did something very important. He cut off the alarm.

Keyes: That was how the men got away. If the alarm had worked, they would not have escaped.

Price: How did you find out about Cross?

Keyes: It was his own fault. At the time he wasn't even a suspect. But he left the bank later that morning and he didn't come back. Perhaps he was afraid. Or perhaps he didn't want to lose his share of the money. We don't know the reason.

Bright: He had left his car near the bank. He joined the others and they divided the money. They each got their share. Young Felstead got four thousand pounds because he only drove the car. Each of the others got twelve thousand pounds.

Driver: When we arrested Jack Felstead, he hadn't spent much of his share. So we got back that part of the money.

Keyes: But when Lessing was arrested, he'd got rid of most of his share. He'd spent a lot of the money on horses.

Bright: We got back a lot of Cross's money. The police saw Cross and Felstead in a car one day and they followed them. They tried to escape but there was an accident and Felstead was killed. We found Cross's money in a bag in the car but we never found Felstead's share.

Price: Didn't Cross know about it?

Bright: Perhaps. But he refused to talk. We searched Felstead's home and Cross's too, but there was no sign of the money.

Keyes: Well, then Cross and Lessing were sent to prison for twelve years. Jack Felstead went to prison for five years.

Price: But now they're all free men.

Keyes: Yes, and now someone's started to use the missing money.

Bright: Clearly someone knows the place where the money was hidden. It may be Cross. He was with Felstead in the car.

Price: Or Jack Felstead. After all, he's the dead man's brother.

Keyes: It may be any one of them. Or perhaps they're all working together. You can see our problem, Price! (*After a moment*) Well, I'll send for some coffee and then we can continue.

Scene 3
(*The four men are drinking their coffee.*)

Keyes: Now let's have the next part of the story.

Bright: I'd like to leave that to Sergeant Driver, sir.

Keyes: Very well. Please continue, Sergeant.

Driver: The man got rid of the stolen money on Monday and he did it like this. He went to ten jewellers' shops and at each he bought a piece of jewellery in five-pound notes—and it was the stolen money, of course.

Keyes: It may seem a lot of trouble to get rid of stolen money but it isn't a bad idea. There are a lot of things you can't buy with stolen money. You have to buy small things.

Bright: The man has got rid of three thousand pounds and in its place he has jewellery. He can hide it easily because the articles are small and when he needs money, he can sell some of them.

Keyes: And he did it all in one day. He may go to another city in a few months' time and do the same thing again. And he may not buy jewellery the next time.

Price: Where were the jewellers' shops?

Bright: Sergeant Driver had better show us on the map.

(*Sergeant Driver gets up and stands in front of the map on the wall. He draws a circle with his finger.*)

Driver: They were all in this area.

Keyes: It's quite a wide area. Clearly the man had a car. He went to all the shops in about five hours, didn't he?

Driver (*sitting down again*): That's right, sir. He started at about ten o'clock and he'd finished by three.

Price: Have you found all the shops? Perhaps there are more.

Bright: No, I'm sure that we've found all of them. We contacted as many jewellers as possible.

Price: How did you find out about this in the first place?

Driver: We were lucky. The next day, some of the jewellers paid their money into their banks. Somebody in one of the banks noticed the stolen money almost immediately.

Keyes: The bank informed us and we started work. We informed other banks and we also contacted the jewellers. In a short time we knew the complete story.

Price: What about the man? If ten jewellers saw him, you must have a very good description of him.

Bright: Yes, we have a good description. (*To Sergeant Driver*) Have you got it there, Sergeant?

Driver: Yes, sir. Here it is. (*He looks at one of his papers and reads from it.*) The man was about fifty years old. He was tall and rather thin. He wore glasses and he had a moustache. He was wearing a dark blue suit and he had a hat on, so nobody noticed the colour of his hair. All the jewellers say he was well dressed. We've made this picture of him.

(*Sergeant Driver gives the picture to Price.*)

Price: Probably the moustache wasn't a real one.

Keyes: I agree. All the jewellers noticed the moustache. That was the man's idea. He wanted them to remember it.

Price: Does he look like any of the men who robbed the bank?

Driver: It's rather difficult to say. Here are their photographs. (*He gives the photographs to Price.*) Of course these photographs were taken many years ago and the men have probably changed a lot. I don't think the man can be Felstead. He's too young. He's still only about thirty-five.

Price: But if he wore a moustache, he'd look older.

Keyes: That's true. I think the man looks like Lessing but Bright thinks he looks like Cross. They're *all* suspects and we must check on all of them.

Bright (*to Sergeant Driver*): How much information have we got, Sergeant? Where do these men live now? What do they do? What about Felstead, for example?

Driver: He has a job in a garage. A little way out of London. On the road to Reading.

Keyes: Has he got into any trouble since he came out of prison?

Driver: No, sir.

Bright: Is he married?

Driver: I don't think he is, but I'm not sure.

Keyes: One of you had better go and see him. What about you, Sergeant Driver?

Driver: I'd rather not go, sir. After all, I arrested him.

Bright: Driver's right. If Felstead remembers him, he may not want to talk. And *I* want to go and see Cross.

Keyes: Well, that leaves Inspector Price.

Price: Very good, sir. Should I just see Felstead, sir, or should I also try to get more information about him?

Keyes: Just go and talk to him. It's much better. If he is honest, we don't want to make trouble for him.

Bright: Good. Then I'll go and see Cross. What happened to him, Sergeant, when he came out of prison?

Driver: Well, his wife went to live with her father. He had a small farm and when he died, he left it to his daughter. Then when Cross came out of prison, he went to live there with his wife. They look after it together. It's about twenty miles south of London, on the road to Brighton. Here's the address, sir. (*He gives Bright a piece of paper.*)

Keyes: Cross hasn't been in trouble either, has he?

Driver: No, sir. He lives a very quiet life. He was a sick man when he came out of prison.

Keyes: Well, that leaves Lessing. (*To Sergeant Driver*) You'd better go and see him, sergeant.

Driver: Very good, sir. Now Lessing *has* been in trouble since he came out of prison.

Keyes: Oh? What's he done?

Driver: He went to prison for three months. I can't remember the reason. Then there was some trouble about a stolen car, but we didn't have enough information to arrest him. But we know he isn't honest.

Price: What does he do?

Driver: I don't know. He used to be an actor before he went to prison. We haven't even got his address at the moment. He doesn't stay in the same place very long. But he's still in London. I know a place where I can find him.

Keyes: Good. Go and question him. Well, I think we've gone over everything. (*The three men stand up.*) Find out all you can and then report to me. Good luck!

(*The three men go out of the room.*)

Act Two

Scene 1

(*A garage on the road to Reading. Inspector Price drives up in his car. He leaves it outside the garage. Price looks around for a moment and then he sees Felstead. Felstead is working on a car. Price goes across to him.*)

Price: Excuse me. I'm having a little trouble with my car. Could you have a look at it for me?

Felstead: Well, we're rather busy at the moment, but if it's only a small job, I'll try to put it right for you.

Price: Thanks very much.

(*Inspector Price leads the way to the car.*)

Felstead: What's the matter with the car?

Price: There isn't anything the matter with the car, in fact. I asked you to come out here because I wanted to talk to you—alone. You *are* Jack Felstead, aren't you?

Felstead: Yes, that's right. Who are *you?*

Price: My name's Price. I'm a police inspector.

Felstead: I see. (*He does not look very pleased.*) But why did you come to the garage? I don't want to lose my job. You could see me at home in the evening. What do you want to see me about?

Price: It'll take a little time to explain. Can't we go for a drive?

Felstead: I'd better ask the man who's in charge of the garage. I'll say I want to test the car.

(*Felstead goes back into the garage. When he returns, both men get into the car. Felstead drives.*)

Felstead: All right. Why do you want to see me? I haven't done anything wrong since I came out of prison. I've tried to live an honest life. Is it about the missing money?

Price: Yes, something's happened and we have to check on you.

Felstead: Well, I don't know anything about it. You got back my share. And I went to prison for five years.

Price: But your brother's share is still missing.

Felstead (*rather angrily*): I don't care. I don't know anything about it. I never saw any of them again.

Price: But your brother hid his money somewhere.

Felstead: He didn't tell me his secrets. Ask one of the others— Lessing or Cross. They were my brother's friends.

Price: Have you seen either of them since you came out of prison?

Felstead: No, I haven't. But . . .

Price: Yes, go on. You'd better tell me.

Felstead: Well, Lessing rang me up about a month ago.

Price: What did he want?

Felstead: He asked to see me. But I refused.

Price: What did he do then? Did he ring off?

Felstead: No. He went on talking, so I put the phone down.

Price: That's an interesting bit of information. It may help us. (*Pause*) Now there's another question I have to ask you. What were you doing on Monday? Were you here at the garage?

Felstead: No, as a matter of fact I wasn't. I . . .

Price: Go on.

Felstead: I didn't come to work on Monday. I worked on Sunday because I had to finish some work on a car which was needed early the next day.

Price: I see. So you had a holiday on Monday. What did you do?

Felstead: I went into London for the day.

Price: By car?

Felstead: Yes, I took my car.

Price: Did you spend all day in London?

Felstead: Yes. You see . . . I'm getting married very soon. I wanted to buy some new clothes. So I did some shopping in the morning and then I went to the cinema in the afternoon.

Price: Were you alone?

Felstead: Yes. Why? Did something happen on Monday?

Price: Yes. But don't worry. We can check your story later.
(*They reach the garage again. Both men get out of the car.*)

Felstead: Listen, Inspector. I've told you all I know. I don't know anything about the missing money. Please believe me.

Price: I believe you. I hope we won't need to trouble you again. Goodbye. And thanks for your help.
(*Felstead goes into the garage. Price gets into his car and drives off.*)

Scene 2

(*Inspector Bright has reached the farm which belongs to Mrs Cross. He goes to the door of the farmhouse and rings the bell. A woman opens the door.*)

Bright: Good afternoon. Are you Mrs Cross?

Mrs Cross: I am.

Bright: I wanted to see your husband. Is he at home?

Mrs Cross: My husband? But he's . . . dead.

Bright: Oh, I'm sorry. (*Pause*) When did he die?

Mrs Cross: In April. He'd been ill for some time.

Bright: Please excuse me. I hadn't heard about it. (*Pause*) Are you looking after the farm by yourself?

Mrs Cross: No, my brother has come to live here and he helps me. You see, it's not a very big place and we have only a few men working on it. Why did you want to see my husband?

Bright: I just wanted to talk to him.

Mrs Cross: Were you a friend of my husband's . . . in the old days?

Bright: Yes. But we hadn't met for several years.

Mrs Cross: You're from the police, aren't you?

Bright: Yes, I am. But since your husband's dead . . .

Mrs Cross: Yes, he's dead—but is that the end of it? He paid for his crime. He spent twelve years in prison and he was a sick man when he came out.

Bright: But we're still looking for the missing money—George Felstead's share of the robbery. Your husband was with Felstead when he was killed in the accident. Perhaps he knew the place where the money was hidden.

Mrs Cross: I can't help you. If he knew about the money, he certainly didn't tell me. We never talked about the robbery.

(*At this moment a man comes towards the farmhouse. He is about fifty years old and is tall and thin.*)

Mrs Cross: Here's my brother. He's come home for his tea. He's been out on the farm most of the day.

(*The man reaches the place where Inspector Bright and Mrs Cross are standing.*)

Woods (*holding out his hand*): How do you do? My name's Woods.

Bright: Mine's Bright. How do you do?

Woods (*to his sister*): Well, Edna, I'm ready for my tea. (*To Bright*)

Won't you come in and join us?

Bright: No, thank you very much. I must go back to London.

Woods: Well, excuse me. I'm really hungry. (*He starts to go into the house. Then he pauses.*) By the way, Edna, I saw some very interesting birds today. I'll tell you about them at tea.

(*Woods goes into the farmhouse.*)

Mrs Cross (*smiling for the first time*): My brother is very interested in birds. Before he came to live on the farm, he used to work in the city. He could only watch birds at weekends and during his holidays. Now he can watch them all the time! He's more interested in birds than he is in the farm! But I'm glad to have him here. He takes charge of the men.

Bright: Well, I must get back to London. I won't trouble you again, Mrs Cross. Good afternoon.

Mrs Cross: Good afternoon.

(*Inspector Bright gets into his car and drives off. Mrs Cross watches him leave. Then her brother comes and joins her at the door.*)

Woods: Who was that?

Mrs Cross: He was from the police. They're still looking for that missing money. After all these years.

Woods (*smiling*): They'll never find it. They ought to forget about it.

(*They both go into the farmhouse.*)

Scene 3

(*In a café. It is early evening. Sergeant Driver is sitting at a table. The waitress has just brought him a pot of tea.*)

Waitress: Here's your tea, sir. (*She puts the tea on the table in front of Driver.*) Would you like anything to eat?

Driver: No, thanks. (*Pause*) Oh, by the way, I'm trying to contact someone. His name's Lessing. Somebody told me he often comes to this café. Do you know him?

Waitress: Why, yes, I do. He eats here quite often in the evening.

Driver: What time does he usually come?

Waitress: About this time. Of course he doesn't come here every evening. In fact I haven't seen him at all this week.

(*The waitress goes off. Driver sits drinking his tea. After a while Lessing comes in and sits at a corner table. He opens a newspaper and begins to read it. Driver gets up and goes across to the table where Lessing is sitting.*)

Driver: Excuse me. Can I have a word with you?

Lessing (*looking up from his newspaper*): What do you want? I don't know you, do I?

Driver: My name's Driver. Sergeant Driver. Perhaps you remember my name.

Lessing (*not very politely*): Yes I remember it—and I remember your face too! So you're a sergeant now!

Driver (*sitting down*): That's enough, Lessing. I just want to ask you a few questions.

Lessing (*putting down his newspaper*): Well, what do the police want now? Why can't they leave me alone? All right, hurry up and ask your questions. I'm hungry and I want to eat.

Driver: It won't take long. What do you do these days, by the way?

Lessing (*taking out a cigarette and lighting it*): I'm a salesman. Surely the police know that.

Driver: You used to be an actor, didn't you?

Lessing: Yes, in the old days. I used to get small parts. But nobody wanted me after I came out of prison.

Driver: But you got a job as a salesman. What do you sell?

Lessing: Cars, second-hand ones. I work for myself. I buy an old car and sell it again. You know the kind of business.

Driver: Where do you work?

Lessing: In London mostly. But I sometimes go out of London if I hear of a good car.

Driver: Is business good?

Lessing (*slowly*): I make enough money.

Driver: What about your friends—Cross, for example?

Lessing (*surprised*): Cross? Haven't you heard? I thought the police knew everything! He died.

Driver: I didn't know that. When did it happen?

Lessing: Several months ago.

Driver: How did you hear about it?

Lessing: Someone told me. It isn't a secret.

Driver: Perhaps not. What about Felstead? Have you seen him?

Lessing: No, I haven't seen *that* young man. (*Lessing laughs but he seems rather afraid.*) He doesn't mix with *us*. But why are you asking me about them?

Driver: We're still looking for that money.

Lessing: The missing money? (*He laughs.*) You'll never find that.

Driver: Why do you say that?

Lessing: Only George Felstead knew where the money was—and he's dead.

Driver: Perhaps he told Cross.

Lessing (*putting out his cigarette*): Perhaps he did. But Cross is dead now, too. (*Pause*) Well, have you got any more questions?

Driver: Just one or two. Where were you last Monday?

Lessing: Last Monday? Well, I was working, of course. In the morning I went to look at a car in south London.

Driver: Did you buy it?

Lessing (*slowly*): No, as a matter of fact I didn't. I liked it but the man wanted too much money for it.

Driver: What time was this?

Lessing: Between nine and ten.

Driver: Well, that isn't a day's work. What did you do after that?

Lessing: I met a friend. We had lunch together and later in the afternoon I went to see another car.

Driver: At what time?

Lessing: It was about four o'clock.

Driver: Did you buy that one?

Lessing: Yes, I did. I made a little money out of it.

Driver: So that was your day's work.

Lessing: Yes, it wasn't a very busy day. Some days are like that.

Driver: Well, I'll have to check your story. Are you sure you don't know anything about the missing money?

Lessing: I've told you. I don't know anything. I'd like to lay my hands on it! Twelve thousand pounds is a lot of money!

Driver: Perhaps. But, remember, it's stolen money. (*He stands up.*) Well, that's all for the moment. But I need your address.

(*Lessing writes his address on a piece of paper and gives it to Driver.*)

Lessing: Here you are. But you can usually find me here in the evening. I'm not at home during the day.

Driver: Don't run away, Lessing.

(*Sergeant Driver goes out of the café. Lessing lights another cigarette. Then he picks up his newspaper and begins to read it again.*)

Act Three

Scene 1

(*The next morning, in the office of Superintendent Keyes. Keyes is sitting behind his desk. Inspector Bright comes in.*)

Keyes: Ah, good morning, Bright. Are the others coming, too?

Bright: They're on their way, sir. They'll be here in a minute.

(*Bright sits down. Inspector Price and Sergeant Driver also come into the office and sit down.*)

Keyes: Good. Now everyone's here. Now, Price, you went to see Felstead, didn't you? What did you find out from him?

Price: Well, I went to the garage, sir. I didn't want to talk to Felstead there, so we went for a ride in my car. I said my car was giving me trouble.

Keyes: Good. What did you think of Felstead?

Price: I think he's honest, sir. He says he knows nothing about the money—and I believe him.

Keyes: That's all very well. But for the moment we have to look at the facts. Where was he on Monday, for example.

Price: In London. He worked on Sunday because he had to finish some work on a car, so he took a holiday the next day.

Keyes: Very interesting! And it happened to be the day when someone got rid of the stolen money!

Price: True, sir, but he didn't know about the holiday until Saturday. So how could he plan to get rid of the money then?

Bright: Perhaps he had the plan ready. How often does he work on Sunday and have a holiday on Monday? Do we know that?

Price: Well, I didn't ask him that.

Keyes: It doesn't matter. What was he doing in London?

Price: He went shopping. He's getting married soon and he wanted to buy some new clothes. After that, he went to the cinema.

Driver: Was he alone in London?

Price: Yes, and he went by car.

Keyes: So in fact Felstead had the opportunity to get rid of the money. He was in London all day and he had a car with him.

Bright: Yes, he certainly had the opportunity. But I don't think Felstead is the man we want. He was very young when he took part in the robbery. Would he make the same mistake again?

Keyes: I hope you're right. But we must look at all the facts. Did you find out anything else?

Price: There was one other thing, sir. Lessing telephoned him a few weeks ago. Lessing wanted to see him, but Felstead refused.

Bright: What did Lessing want?

Price: Felstead doesn't know. He didn't want to talk to Lessing.

Keyes (*to Sergeant Driver*): Did Lessing mention this to you?

Driver: I asked him about Felstead, but he only laughed. But he seemed afraid when I mentioned Felstead's name.

Keyes: I see. What did you find out from Lessing?

Driver: Well, I met him in a café and we talked for some time. But he wasn't very friendly.

Bright: What does he do these days?

Driver: He's a salesman. He buys and sells second-hand cars.

Keyes: That's very interesting. And where was he on Monday?

Driver: He was working. He went to south London in the morning to look at a car. Then he had lunch with a friend and went to see another car in the afternoon.

Bright: Well, he had plenty of opportunity to get rid of the money and he probably knows all the jewellers' shops in London.

Keyes: We must certainly watch Lessing.

Bright: I've already taken care of that. In fact, I'm not taking any chances. I've sent men to watch both Felstead and Lessing. We're watching the farm too. But since Cross is dead—

Keyes (*surprised*): Dead? When did this happen?

Bright: Several months ago. Mrs Cross still runs the farm, with some help from her brother.

Keyes: What do you think of her?

Bright: She's not the sort of woman who would do this.

Price: If Cross knew about the money, perhaps he told someone before he died.

Driver: Lessing, perhaps. Lessing knew that Cross was dead.

Keyes: So Lessing was still in touch with Cross. If Lessing knew about the money, he would want to use it. So perhaps he telephoned Felstead for that reason. He wanted his help.

Price: But who went into the jewellers' shops? The man didn't look like Lessing, either.

Keyes: Well, I've got one more piece of information for you. (*Pause.*) While you were out yesterday, one of the banks telephoned. They've found some more stolen money.

Bright: How much?

Keyes: One five-pound note. But it's part of the stolen money.

Bright: Where did it come from? One of the jewellers' shops?

Keyes: No, that's the interesting thing. It came from a bookseller. I've got the name and address here. (*He looks at a piece of paper.*) Thomas Lamb and Son, Little Wall Street. I's quite near one of the jewellers' shops in fact.

Bright: Well, we'd better go and see the bookseller.

(*At that moment the telephone rings. Keyes picks it up.*)

Keyes: Hello? Yes, Superintendent Keyes here. Gone? Are you sure? When did this happen? ... I see. Which way did he go? South? ... All right. We'll do something at once.

(*Keyes puts down the telephone.*)

Bright: Who's gone, sir? Lessing?

Keyes: No, Felstead! He didn't go to the garage this morning. He took his car and went south. He took the Brighton road.

Price: Then he went towards the farm.

Keyes: It looks like it. Well, we'd better go after him. I'll come too. Things are beginning to happen at last!

Bright: What about the bookseller?

Keyes: Yes, we mustn't forget him. It may still be important. Inspector Price, you go and see the bookseller. Then come down to the farm and join us there. We may need your help.

Price: Very good, sir.

Keyes (*to Bright*): We'll need a car. We'll leave in ten minutes.

(*The three men stand up and go out of the office.*)

Scene 2

(*In the shop of Mr Thomas Lamb, the bookseller. Mr Lamb is sitting behind the counter, reading. When Inspector Price comes in, he puts away the book and stands up.*)

Mr Lamb: Good morning, sir.

Price: I'm from the police. My name's Price. Inspector Price.

Mr Lamb (*looking worried*): The police! I haven't done anything wrong, have I?

Price (*smiling*): I don't think so, Mr Lamb. But I've got to ask you a few questions.

Mr Lamb: Well, come into the office at the back of the shop.

(*Inspector Price follows Mr Lamb into the small office behind the shop.*)

Price: Well, Mr Lamb, I've come to ask you about a five-pound note which you paid into your bank yesterday. Can you remember the customer who gave it to you?

Mr Lamb: A five-pound note? I'd better look in my book. I keep a record of the money I take to the bank. (*He takes a book out of his desk.*) Let me see. Yes, I paid four five-pound notes and twenty-two one-pound notes into my bank. There was some small change, too. Now the question is: where did the five-pound notes come from? Let me think.

Price: I may be able to help a little. I telephoned the bank and they say that three of the notes are new. And the numbers on each of the notes followed one another, so that they probably all came from the same person.

Mr Lamb: Ah, yes! I remember now. I got those three notes from Mr Lee on Tuesday. Mr Lee is another bookseller. He bought some books from me for one of his customers.

Price: Good. That leaves only one five-pound note. Only one—but that's the one which interests us. Think hard!

(*There is a pause while Mr Lamb tries to remember.*)

Mr Lamb: I'm very sorry. I just can't remember.

Price: I may be able to help again. (*He takes a piece of paper out of his pocket.*) Here is a picture of a man we are trying to find. A lot of people saw him and we have drawn this picture from the description which they gave us.

Mr Lamb (*looking hard at the picture*): His face seems familiar.

Price: He was tall and rather thin. He was wearing a dark blue suit and he had a hat on. He probably came into your shop on Monday. In the afternoon perhaps, but we're not sure.

Mr Lamb (*thinking*): Wait a minute! Yes, I remember now. (*He takes out a big notebook and opens it.*) Yes, you're quite right. It was Monday. Someone bought a new book for seven pounds.

Price: Good. Can you tell me anything about the man? How long did he spend in your shop?

Mr Lamb: Oh, nearly half an hour. He didn't seem in a hurry. He asked to see the books which I had about birds. In fact I haven't got many. I showed them to him but they didn't interest him very much. Then I remembered another book. I bought it specially for a customer but in the end the man didn't buy it. It's a book about water birds. It's not a new book and it's rather difficult to get a copy these days.

Price: Was this the book that you sold him?

Mr Lamb: Yes, it was. As soon as he saw it, the man wanted it. It's a very beautiful book.

Price: And he paid you with the five-pound note?

Mr Lamb: Yes, I'm quite sure of that now. You see, at first the man thought he hadn't enough money. The book cost seven pounds and the man had only five pounds. Then he said: "I've got some more money. I was going to do some shopping but I've changed my mind. I'll take the book instead." So he took this money from another pocket and paid me with a five-pound note.

Price: Well, that's all very interesting. So it was the same man who came here. And he bought a book about birds. (*He stands up.*) Thank you, Mr Lamb. You've helped us quite a lot.

Mr Lamb (*also standing up*): But what's it all about, Inspector?

Price: I'm afraid I can't tell you that now. When we catch the man, you'll be able to read about it in the newspaper.

(*Inspector Price goes back into the shop. Mr Lamb follows him.*)

Price: Good morning, Mr Lamb. Thank you again.

Mr Lamb: Good morning, Inspector.

(*Inspector Price goes out of the shop.*)

Scene 3

(*A place not far from Mrs Cross's farm. Keyes, Bright, Driver and a village policeman are there. They have found Felstead's car.*)

Village policeman: We saw him as soon as he reached the village, sir. We had the number of his car. Felstead got out of his car and went into the post office. He asked for the address of the farm. Then he went up to the farm and we followed him.

Keyes: That's interesting. So he didn't know the address of the farm. What did he do when he arrived there?

Village policeman: He rang the bell. Mrs Cross came to the door and they talked for some time.

Bright: Didn't Felstead go into the farm?

Village policeman: No, sir. We were watching him all the time.

Keyes: Did Felstead seem angry when he talked to Mrs Cross?

Village policeman: No, sir. They both talked very quietly. They didn't shout or quarrel. Then after some time, Felstead left.

Bright: It's very strange. What did Felstead want?

Keyes: He wanted to see Cross. He didn't know Cross was dead.

Bright: Yes, that must be the answer. But what's Felstead doing now?

Is he looking for something?

Village policeman: Well, when he left the farm, he drove down this road, I thought he was returning to London. But instead he stopped his car here and got out. Then he began to walk across the fields and he hasn't come back. That was almost half an hour ago.

Keyes: Well, he'll come back. We'll wait for him here.

Driver (*suddenly*): Look, sir! He's coming now. (*He points across the fields.*)

Keyes: Yes, that's him. We'd better hide. (*He points to some bushes near Felstead's car.*) We can wait behind those bushes.

(*The policemen hide behind the bushes. Felstead comes slowly across the field. When he reaches his car, the policemen rush out.*)

Felstead: What's all this? Have the police come to meet me?

Keyes: That's right, Felstead. But we'll ask the questions. What are you doing here? Why did you go to the farm?

Felstead: I went to see Cross.

Bright: Did you expect to get money from him?

Felstead: No, that wasn't the reason. It's like this. I took part in the robbery many years ago. I went to prison and I thought I could forget about that part of my life. But some of the money is still missing and now someone has started to use it. And I'm one of the suspects. Isn't that true?

Keyes: Yes, you *are* one of the suspects.

Felstead: Well, after Inspector Price came to see me, I asked myself: how long will this continue? I live an honest life—but the police still watch me. I'm getting married soon. The girl I'm going to marry doesn't know about my past. I don't *want* her to know about it. So I wanted to put an end to this. For that reason I came to the farm. I wanted to speak to Cross.

Bright: But what did you expect to do? Did Cross know about the money?

Felstead: I don't know. But it's possible, isn't it? He was with my brother when he died. I intended to lie to Cross. I was going to say: "The money belonged to my brother and I want a share of it. If you don't give me my share, I'll go to the police."

Bright: But would Cross have listened to you?

Felstead: I think so. He was very fond of my brother. Perhaps he would have given me a share of the money if he had had it.

Keyes: What would you have done then?

Felstead: If he had given me some of the money, I would have gone to the police. I promise you.

Keyes: Well, Cross is dead. You know that, don't you?

Felstead: Yes, his wife told me. She doesn't know anything about the money. I'm sure of that. But, I discovered one thing. Lessing has been down here. He came before Cross died and he came again after that. He was after the money. When he telephoned me, I think he wanted me to help him.

Keyes: Yes, that's possible. But has Lessing got the money?

Felstead: I don't know. Mrs Cross couldn't help me.

Bright: But what were you doing in the fields?

Felstead (*surprised, but he laughs*): Nothing! I started to go back to the village. But then I changed my mind. It's a lovely day and I decided to go for a walk. That's all!

(*At that moment Inspector Price arrives in his car. He gets out and comes across to the group.*)

Price: So you've got Felstead.

Keyes: Yes, but he isn't the man we want. What did you find out at the bookshop?

Price: Not much, sir. But it was the same man who went to the jewellers' shops. The bookseller recognised his picture.

Keyes: What did he buy in the bookshop?

Price: He bought a book about birds.

Keyes: Birds!

Price: Yes, sir. He bought an expensive book about birds.

Keyes: Well, that doesn't help us much.

Bright (*suddenly*): But it does, sir! I think I know the man we're looking for.

Keyes: I don't understand, Bright. *How* do you know?

Bright: I'd better explain, sir. When I went to the farm to see Cross, I met his wife and I also met her brother, Woods.

Keyes: Yes, you mentioned that.

Bright: But I didn't mention something else. At the time it didn't seem important. (*Pause*) Mrs Cross's brother is very interested in birds! He spends his time watching them.

Keyes: But does he look like the man who went to the jewellers' shops?

Bright: Yes, he does! I can see that now, but I didn't notice it at the time. He's tall and thin and he's about fifty years old. He has a moustache too. But when I saw him he was wearing old clothes, and he looked quite different from the man who went to the jewellers' shops.

Keyes: Then we'd better go and see Mr . . . what did you say his name is?

Bright: Woods.

Keyes: We'll go to the farm at once. Felstead, you had better go to the village and wait at the police station. We can't let you go yet. (*He turns to the village policeman.*) You can go with him in his car.

Village policeman: Very good, sir.

(*Keyes goes in the car with Inspector Price. Bright and Driver get into the other car. The village policeman gets into Felstead's car. They all drive off.*)

Scene 4

(*Superintendent Keyes and his men reach the farmhouse. Inspector Bright rings the bell and Mrs Cross opens the door.*)

Bright: Good afternoon, Mrs Cross. I called to see you yesterday.

Mrs Cross: Yes, Inspector. What is it now?

Bright: We've come to see your brother. Is he in?

Mrs Cross: Yes. He's just come back for a cup of tea. Shall I call him?

Bright: We'd rather come in if it's not any trouble.

(*Mrs Cross leads the way into the house. She takes them to the sitting room. Woods is there drinking his tea.*)

Woods: Oh, good afternoon. (*He stands up.*) You're the man who called yesterday, aren't you? (*To Inspector Bright.*)

Bright: That's correct. And this is Superintendent Keyes.

Woods: How do you do?

Mrs Cross: I'll bring you all some tea.

Keyes: Thank you very much.

(*Mrs Cross goes out of the room.*)

Woods: Well, please sit down, gentlemen. (*They all sit down.*) Now, what can I do to help you?

Bright: We want to ask you a few questions.

Woods: Me? What do you want to know?

Bright: First of all, where were you on Monday?

Woods (*surprised*): Why, I was here, of course. On the farm.

Bright: Are you sure? Didn't you leave the farm at all?

Woods: No, I was here all the time.

Keyes: Can you prove that?

Woods: Yes, I can prove it. My sister will tell you.

Keyes: What about the men who work on the farm. Didn't they see you?

Woods: Yes. At least they saw me in the morning.

Bright: At what time?

Woods: When we started work at seven-thirty.

Bright: Didn't anyone else see you after that?

Woods: Well, I was working alone for most of the day. I was on another part of the farm. Perhaps someone saw me during the day. I can't remember.

Bright: Hm. That doesn't help us very much. Are you sure you didn't go to London that day?

Woods: Yes, quite sure. I didn't leave the farm.

Price: Mr Woods, you're very interested in birds, aren't you?

Woods: Yes, that's quite right. But there's nothing wrong in that, is there? I've been interested in birds all my life.

Price: Do you buy books about birds?

Woods: Yes, I do. I've got quite a large number.

Price: Have you ever been to the shop of Thomas Lamb in Little Wall Street?

Woods: No, I don't even know the shop.

Price: We believe you went there on Monday afternoon.

Woods: But, gentlemen, I told you. I didn't even leave the farm on Monday. But what is all this about?

(*At this moment Mrs Cross comes in with the tea.*)

Woods: Edna, these gentlemen want to know where I was on Monday. Please tell them.

Mrs Cross: My brother was here, of course. He didn't leave the farm that day. What is all this about? Why are you asking my brother all these questions.

(*The three policemen look at one another.*)

Keyes: I'll tell you. On Monday a man got rid of three thousand pounds of stolen money. It was the money which your husband and the others stole from the bank years ago. We have a good description of the man—and he looks like your brother.

(*Inspector Price takes out the picture of the man and shows it to Mrs Cross and Woods.*)

Woods (*surprised*): Yes! The man *does* look like me. My moustache is like this and I wear the same kind of glasses.

Keyes: The man was also tall and thin and he was about the same age as you are.

Woods: But I never left the farm on Monday!

Mrs Cross: You'd all better have your cup of tea!

Keyes: Yes, we need it!

(*They all sit drinking tea for a short time. Nobody speaks.*)

Keyes: Now, Mr Woods. You say that you never left the farm on Monday. But a man like you went to London and visited about twenty jewellers' shops. He also went to Thomas Lamb and bought an expensive book about birds. He used the stolen money in the jewellers' shops and he used it in the bookshop too. These are the facts of the case. (*He turns to Mrs Cross.*) Your husband probably knew about that money—but now he's dead. If I believe your brother's story, what is the explanation? We must find one. Either your brother went to London and got rid of the money, or it was someone who looked like your brother.

Price (*suddenly*): Just a moment, sir. I think I can find an explanation. (*He turns to Sergeant Driver.*) Sergeant Driver, you went to see Lessing yesterday. How old is he now?

Driver: Oh, he's about fifty, sir. He looks rather younger perhaps.

Price: Is he also tall and thin?

Driver: Yes, sir. Like Mr Woods here.

Price: But he hasn't got a moustache, has he?

Driver: No, sir. No moustache. And he doesn't wear glasses.

Price: Good. (*He turns to Woods.*) Now, Woods, have you met Lessing?

(*Woods and Mrs Cross look at each other.*)

Woods: Yes, I have. I—

Mrs Cross: He came to the house before my husband died. My husband was ill at the time. Lessing heard about it and came to see him.

Price: Were they alone together?

Mrs Cross: Yes. I couldn't stay with them all the time.

Price (*to Woods*): Did you meet Lessing then?

Woods: Yes, I did. I had just come to live on the farm. My sister needed help because her husband was ill.

Price: Did you talk very much to Lessing?

Woods: No. But then he came again, a few weeks ago.

Price: When Lessing came the second time, did he ask you many questions about yourself.

Woods (*surprised*): Yes, he did. He asked me rather a lot of questions. It seemed strange at the time because I didn't know the man very well.

Price: What sort of questions did he ask?

Woods: He asked me about my job in London, before I came to work on the farm.

Price: What was your job, Mr Woods? Were you a jeweller?

Woods (*surprised*): Yes, I was! But how did you know that?

Price: It was just an idea I had. So Lessing knew you worked in a jeweller's shop.

Woods: He was also very interested in my bird-watching. He asked me a lot of questions about that.

Price: And you told him all he wanted to know.

Woods: Of course! I'm always ready to talk about birds!

Price (*pleased*): Well, now I think that we have the explanation. We'd all forgotten one thing. Lessing used to be an actor. He wasn't a very good one, perhaps, but he was good enough to become Mr Woods for one day. When Lessing met Mr Woods, he noticed that they were the same age. They were also both thin and tall. Lessing only needed a moustache and a pair of glasses and he really looked like Woods. Then he began to make his plans carefully. He wanted Woods to be the suspect, so he decided to use jewellers' shops. But that wasn't enough for Lessing. He also went to a bookshop and bought a book about birds. The bookshop was quite near one of the jewellers' shops. He wanted the bookseller to remember him, so he spent quite a long time in the shop. With all these facts we ought to arrest Woods!

Woods: I'm glad you believe me!

Mrs Cross: But where did Lessing get the stolen money?

Keyes: I'm afraid your husband told him about it, Mrs Cross. This is the only explanation. He knew all these years. He didn't tell you about the money because he knew that you didn't want it. But he told his old friend Lessing.

Bright (*to Mrs Cross*): May I use your telephone?

Mrs Cross: Yes, of course.

Bright (*to Keyes*): I'll telephone Scotland Yard, sir. They had better go and arrest Lessing at once.

Keyes (*smiling*): Don't worry, Inspector. When Felstead ran off this morning, I didn't take any chances. Before I left, I had Lessing arrested. So he's now safely in our hands!

Stress and intonation exercises

Introductory note

These exercises in the Structural Readers (Play Series) Stage 3–6 cover step by step some of the basic features of stress and intonation in English. If they are done carefully and practised regularly, they will help to improve the students' reading aloud.

In a typical English sentence, only words that are important for the meaning are stressed: that is, they are said more loudly and therefore heard more clearly. These words, for the most part, are nouns, main verbs, adjectives and adverbs. Here are some examples with the stressed words or syllables marked like this:

1 She 'gave him a 'book for his 'birthday.
2 'John has 'borrowed some 'money.
3 I 'didn't 'know that she had re'fused to 'do it.

There is one very important thing to notice: stressed syllables are said with a fairly regular beat, and the lightly stressed syllables that come between them are hurried over to maintain that beat. For example, each of these sentences takes about the same length of time to say, because they all have the same number of stressed syllables.

1 'John 'drinks 'milk.
2 'Tom has 'cut his 'hand.
3 'Fred has been 'cutting the 'grass.
4 'Mary has been 'looking at my 'book.

Intonation is the tune with which an utterance is said. In general, the voice falls or rises on the last important stressed syllable in the sentence. Stressed syllables before the fall or rise are said on a level note, starting high and descending stepwise. Here are some examples.

1 TUNE 1 (FALL)

'Mary 'gave her 'brother a 'book.

2 TUNE 2 (RISE)

'Did she 'give him a 'new ,pen?

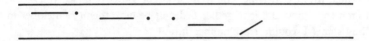

If there are any unstressed syllables before the first stressed syllable, these are said on a low note. Unstressed syllables after the fall are also said on a low note.

3 I'm 'going to 'give you a 'book for your ` birthday.

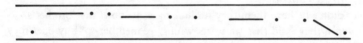

If there are any unstressed syllables after the rise, the voice continues to go up on these.

4 'Will you 'come to ,town with me?

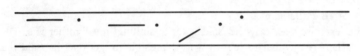

Statements, commands and questions beginning with a word like *What...? When...?* are generally said with a falling intonation. Requests and questions beginning with an auxiliary verb like *Did...? Can...?* are usually said with a rising intonation.

Procedure The teacher should first read the practice sentences aloud to the class. Then the students, either individually or in groups, should repeat each sentence after the teacher. If the initial practice is in chorus, this should be followed up with some individual practice.

Exercise 1 Each of these sentences contains six syllables. At the head of each group the stress pattern is shown: stressed syllables are indicated by a big X and lightly stressed syllables by a small x. Repeat each sentence three times after your teacher.

a) *Stress Pattern:* x X x x x X

they're 'looking at it ` now/ he 'kept it for a ` week/ I 'haven't any ` ink/ the 'exercise was ` wrong/ re'member my ad ` dress/it's 'difficult to ` find/ it 'wasn't a sur ` prise/she 'gave me some to ` day/they 'said that we were ` wrong/ I 'think that he's a ` fraid.

49

b) *Stress Pattern:* x X x x X x

He's 'written a 'story/it 'isn't ex'citing/ the 'rest of them 'liked it/I 'wanted to 'meet her/the 'children have got some/we'll 'see you to'morrow/ they 'did it to'gether/I 'didn't be'lieve them/ re'member to 'buy some/ I 'couldn't pro'nounce it.

c) *Stress Pattern:* x X x X x x

the 'doctor 'gave him some/they 'went on 'holiday/their 'house was 'wonderful/ we 'took some 'photographs/he 'didn't 'practise it/ you 'mustn't 'laugh at him/my 'brother's 'eaten it/per'haps it's 'possible/the 'waiter 'brought them some/they 'haven't sent me one.

d) *Mixed Patterns*

we 'didn't be'lieve them/they're 'looking at it 'now/ my 'brother's 'eaten it/they 'said that we were 'wrong/ re'member to 'buy one/ they 'didn't 'speak to her/ the 'prisoners es'caped/ she 'said that she was 'ill/ I 'did it on 'Friday/ we 'saw the ac'cident.

Exercise 2 Each of these sentences contains seven syllables. Repeat each sentence three times after your teacher.

a) *Stress Pattern:* x X x x x X x

the 'exercise was 'easy/ he 'sold it for a 'shilling/ my 'brother is a 'teacher/ re'member to re'turn it /it's 'possible to 'get one/ he 'said that he for'got it/they 'cannot under'stand it/they 'said that they be'lieved me/the 'story was ex'citing/ the 'photograph's fa'miliar.

b) *Stress Pattern:* x X x x X x x

she's 'eaten the 'oranges /I 'showed him the 'dictionary/ they 'wanted to 'look at it/the 'garden was 'wonderful/ you 'promised to 'give me one/ they're 'travelling by 'aeroplane/ per'haps he's a'shamed of it/ I 'wanted to 'show you one/she 'didn't re'member me.

c) *Mixed Patterns*

I 'wanted to 'show you one/the 'story was ex'citing/the 'garden was 'wonderful/ it's 'possible to 'get one/ we 'noticed it 'yesterday/ the 'telephone was 'ringing/he 'promised to re'turn it /she 'said that she 'wanted them/ they 'may be a'shamed of it.

Exercise 3 Each of these sentences contains eight syllables. Repeat each sentence three times after your teacher.

a) *Stress Pattern:* x X x x X x x X

re'member to 'buy me some 'fruit/ they've 'almost de'cided to 'go/ the 'children were 'walking to 'school/ it 'wasn't ex'citing to 'watch/ the 'book that you 'borrowed was 'mine/ they 'didn't have 'time to

es'cape/the 'dress she was 'wearing was ' new/ the 'bicycle 'wasn't his
'own/per'haps you have 'left it be' hind.
b) *Stress Pattern:* x X x X x X x x
I 'sent a 'letter ' yesterday/ you'll 'have to 'take some 'photographs/
we've 'never 'even 'heard of him/ they 'didn't 'see the 'accident/ the
'test he 'set was 'difficult/ we 'sometimes 'used to ' visit them/ you
'know that 'milk is 'good for you/I 'didn't 'want to 'show them one/
they 'promised 'not to 'play with it.
c) *Mixed Patterns*
they've 'almost de'cided to 'go/I 'didn't 'want to 'show them one/ the
'dress she was 'wearing was 'new/ the 'test he 'set was 'difficult/ she
'said that the 'house was on ' fire/ I 'hope to 'find a ' better one/ she
'quarrelled with 'most of her 'friends/ the 'picture 'didn't interest
him/ the 'students have 'promised to 'help.

*Exercise 4 Falling intonation (mixed statements, question-word questions
and commands). Repeat each sentence three times after your teacher, letting your voice fall on the syllable marked'.*
per'haps he'wants a'nother/'get a 'better 'dictionary/ 'where did the
'aeroplane ' land?/how 'long did you 'spend in the ' library?/ it was
'difficult to 'follow the conver'sation/'don't 'break my um'brella/
'write the 'letter im'mediately/ it's a 'photograph of my 'sister's ' chil-
dren/'why did you 'walk in the 'middle of the ' road?/'when were the
'new ma'chines de'livered?/ you'd 'better 'telephone for the 'doctor/
'who ' saw the 'accident yesterday?/ the 'waiter 'dropped the 'plate he
was carrying.

*Exercise 5 Repeat this dialogue after your teacher. Then learn it by heart
and practise saying it without looking at the text.*
A I've 'just 'bought a 'camera.
B 'Let me 'have a 'look at it. ' Yes, it's 'very ' nice. How 'much did
   you ' pay for it?
A 'Only 'five 'pounds. But it 'wasn't 'new. I ' got it from a ' friend.
B Well, 'now you can 'take some 'photographs.
A I'll 'take one 'now. 'Come into the ' garden.
B 'Where shall I ' stand?
A 'Over ' there. With the 'tree be'hind you.
B I'm ' ready.
A ' Good. 'Don't move. I'm 'just going to ' take it.

Exercise 6 Rising intonation. Repeat each sentence three times after your teacher. Say the question with a rising intonation on the syllable marked, and the response with a single fall on the auxiliary word.

a) 'Do you 'want a'nother 'cup of ,coffee?   'Yes, I 'do.
b) 'Did the 'train 'leave on ,time?   'Yes, it `did.
c) 'Has she 'taken her ,medicine?   'No, she `hasn't.
d) 'Was the 'film ,interesting?   'Yes, it` was.
e) 'Did you 'see the 'accident your,self?   'No, I `didn't.
f) 'Were there any ,letters today?   'No, there `weren't.
g) 'Did the 'suit ,cost very much?   'Yes, it `did.

Exercise 7 Rising intonation. Requests. Repeat each sentence after your teacher, letting your voice rise on the syllable marked,.
'please ,help me/ 'please 'don't 'read my ,letters/' leave it on the ,table, please /'please 'bring it ,back/ 'give me 'fifty ,pence/ 'come a little ,nearer/ 'try to 'work ,harder/'have a 'look at this re,port/ 'don't be a,fraid of me/ 'do en,joy yourselves.

Exercise 8 Rising intonation. Echo questions. Repeat each sentence three times after your teacher. Say both the question beginning with an auxiliary verb and the echo question with a rising intonation as marked. Say the response with double falling intonation as marked.
a) 'Is this ,gold? ,Gold? 'No, it ` isn't.
b) 'Is there a ,garage near here? A ,garage? 'No, there ` isn't.
c) 'Was her ,husband there? Her ,husband? 'No, he `wasn't.
d) 'Have you 'seen my ,dictionary? Your ,dictionary? 'No, I `haven't.
e) 'Was she a,shamed of herself? A,shamed? 'No, she ` wasn't.
f) 'Is he ,lazy? ,Lazy? ' No, I 'don't 'think so.
g) 'Did he ,kiss her? ,Kiss her? ` Yes, I 'think so.

Exercise 9 Rising intonation (in the subordinate clause) + falling intonation (in the main clause). Repeat each sentence three times after your teacher.
a) 'When they ,left, it was 'raining `hard.
b) 'If you 'can't under,stand me, I'll 'speak more slowly.
c) As 'soon as she 'got the ,letter, she was `happy.
d) 'If you ,hurry, you'll 'catch the `train.
e) 'When you ,find it, 'leave it on my table.